GROOMING

by

Susan McBane

Illustrations by

Carole Vincer

THRESHOLD BOOKS

First published in Great Britain by
Threshold Books, The Kenilworth Press Limited
Addington, Buckingham, MK18 2JR

Reprinted 1993

Typeset by DP Photosetting, Aylesbury, Bucks

Printed in Great Britain by Westway Offset

CONTENTS

Introduction

Grooming is one of the hardest physical jobs involved in caring for a horse or pony. If you're giving your pony a full grooming and you aren't fit yourself, you may well feel you'll never last out till the horse is finished. But, like any activity where physical fitness is involved, the more often you do it the fitter you become and the less you notice the hard work. And it is very rewarding to stand back and look at a smart, clean horse and know it was all your own work.

This is just as well because grooming is important in keeping the pony's skin and coat healthy and clean and able to work efficiently. His skin and coat help to protect him from the outside world, to expel poisons in his sweat, keep warm *and* to cool down. Through nerves in his skin, he is aware of cold, heat, pressure, pleasure and pain.

The skin is made of two main layers: an outer layer of dead cells constantly flaking off and seen as dandruff in the coat, and an inner, sensitive layer which constantly replaces the outer layer. There are also oil glands in the skin, giving out natural oil (sebum) which helps lubricate the skin and coat and makes them water-resistant.

Wild horses and those living out need some dirt and grease in their coats for protection against the weather; rain removes the excess. Stabled horses need us to keep them clean and stimulate their skins by grooming as they are denied a lot of mutual grooming with teeth, rubbing and rolling which more naturally living horses enjoy.

Grooming also builds up trust (or lack of it!) between horse and owner, giving a chance for close contact and an automatic thorough daily inspection.

Benefits of grooming

It's amazing what a difference grooming makes to a horse's appearance. On the left below is a nicely groomed, clean, smart-looking horse and, on the right, the same horse dirty, ungroomed and looking uncared-for.

Grooming not only helps the horse to look good, but also helps to keep him healthy. Skin parasites such as lice love a dirty environment with plenty of organic debris such as grease, flakes of dead skin and dried sweat, which some of them feed on. An undisturbed home makes it easy for them to lay eggs and for their young to flourish.

Keeping your horse reasonably clean shows that you respect him and the horse world in general. Dirty, scruffy horses and riders earn themselves a bad name.

It's not very pleasant riding a filthy, greasy horse – you'll soon get dirty, so will his tack and clothing.

With a grass-kept horse you may feel it's not worth the effort of getting him clean because as soon as he goes back to his field he'll roll, and, especially if the ground is muddy, all your hard work will be undone – but this is only partly true. You should still want to look fairly respectable when you ride, and a regular light grooming helps to avoid a build-up of thick grease, dandruff and dirt on grass-kept horses, especially in dry weather when there's no rain to remove any of it.

Regular (daily) full or part grooming also means you're more likely to spot wounds and skin disorders which could otherwise become more serious and difficult to clear up – so there's every reason to keep your horse, stabled or at grass, properly groomed for his lifestyle.

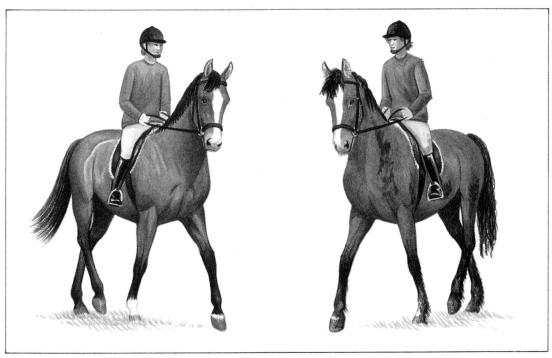

Basic kit

A basic grooming kit has enough tools to keep your horse clean on a daily basis. If you're just starting off you can buy other items later. A basic kit comprises: dandy brush, body brush, metal curry comb, hoof pick and two fairly small or flat sponges in different colours.

The **dandy brush** may have a strong wooden or plastic back and stiff, fairly long bristles, either natural bristle or plastic. Natural bristle is by far the best as the ends do not split, flatten and become useless. Split bristles also catch and tear the mane and tail hairs and become easily tangled with hair. The dandy brush is used for removing dried mud and manure (politely called 'stable stains'!).

The **body brush** is oval-shaped, again with a wooden or plastic back, although the best and easiest to use are leather backed. These latter mould to your hand, are lighter and don't hurt the horse if you accidentally knock him. Body brushes have shorter, finer bristles (again, natural bristle is best) and a leather, canvas or plastic loop over the back for your hand to slip into, making the brush easier and firmer to use.

The body brush is used to remove grease, dandruff and general dirt from not only the body coat but also the skin and is recommended for use on manes (including the forelock) and tails, being gentler than the dandy brush. It is also used on the roots of the mane and tail hair.

The **metal curry comb** is for cleaning the body brush, *not the horse*; the **hoof pick** for cleaning out under the feet, and the **sponges** for cleaning eyes, nostrils, sheath and dock. Use one colour for the front end and the other for the back end – and never mix them up.

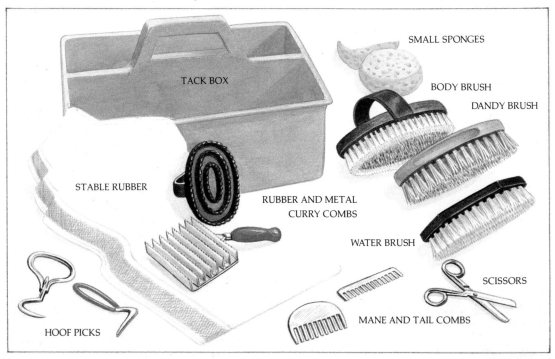

SMALL SPONGES

TACK BOX

BODY BRUSH

DANDY BRUSH

STABLE RUBBER

RUBBER AND METAL CURRY COMBS

WATER BRUSH

SCISSORS

HOOF PICKS

MANE AND TAIL COMBS

Full kit

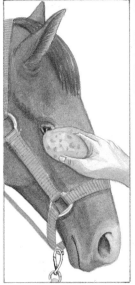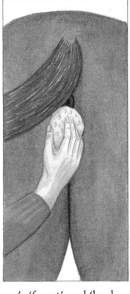

Damp-sponging the horse's 'front' and 'back ends' keeps these sensitive parts clean and refreshes him. Dry him with a stable rubber in cold weather.

To make up a full kit you can add: a **water brush** (for laying or damping down the mane, forelock and tail); **rubber and plastic curry combs** for removing dried mud and stable stains from the horse and helping to remove loose hairs; a **stable rubber** (like a tea towel) for a final polish over; a **cactus cloth** (good for removing surface dirt and hairs); a **sweat scraper** for removing sweat or water; a **plastic pan-scrub** for removing dried mud; an old **silk scarf** for putting a shine on the coat; and a **mane comb** and **scissors** for trimming mane, forelock, tail, fetlocks, under the jaw and the edges of the ears (although, strictly speaking, this is not part of ordinary grooming).

You'll notice that hoof oil is not advised. Scientific research is showing that ordinary hoof oils are not absorbed and can prevent the evaporation of excess moisture in wet weather.

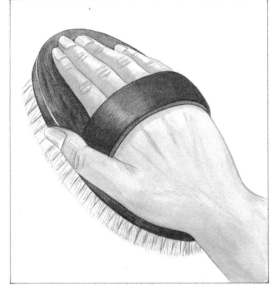

Hold your body brush like this, with your thumb on the outside of the strap.

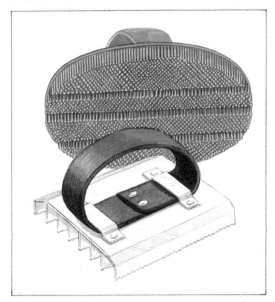

A plastic-toothed curry comb (top) should be used gently as it can scratch. The metal curry comb shown has a loop instead of the more usual wooden handle.

On a short coat, a cactus cloth of rough natural fibre is good for a quick, firm rub-down to remove surface dirt and loose hairs and stimulate the skin.

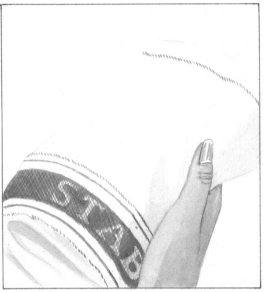

The stable rubber removes dust which may have settled on the groomed coat and gives a final polish. You can also cover your kit-holder with it.

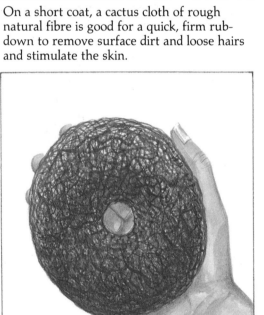

A plastic pan-scrub is good for removing dried mud and stains and won't annoy a sensitive horse as might a dandy brush or plastic comb.

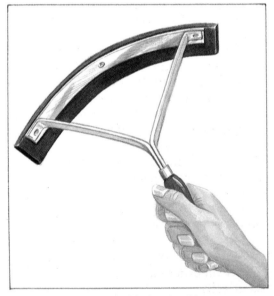

A sweat scraper is a blade of rubber on a metal frame, with a wooden handle. It removes excess water (rain, sweat or rinsing water) like a windscreen wiper.

Electrical gadgets

There are clipping and grooming machines to help you keep your horse looking smart with less effort.

In winter, horses and ponies who are working hard have at least some of their long body coat clipped off so they don't sweat too much and lose body condition (weight).

Electric clippers do a good job if the blades are kept clean and sharp and at the correct tension. You'll need a properly earthed plug and socket (or cable extension) with a circuit breaker for safety. Keep excess flex in a dry rubber or plastic bucket (not metal or with a metal handle) or a washing-up bowl, so the horse is less likely to tread on it. The person clipping should wear rubber boots or shoes, again for safety in case of shocks.

If you're inexperienced, pay a professional to give you a clipping lesson, and clip your horse or pony under expert supervision. Otherwise, pay someone experienced to clip for you.

Clipping makes the horse easier to keep clean but the more you clip off the more food and clothing he'll need.

Grooming machines really save hard work! The best combine vacuuming with a cylindrical brush-head which whizzes round and flicks the dirt into a tube, down which the dirt is sucked into a container, like a domestic vacuum cleaner.

The same safety precautions apply when electric-grooming as when clipping.

A weekly or twice-weekly electric groom means you can groom more lightly on other days as the machines are so effective.

With the rotary-brush type, be careful not to entangle the mane and tail hairs.

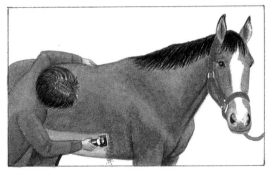

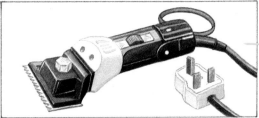

Lightweight, cool-running clippers are easy to use and less likely to worry the horse. Many dislike the noise and vibration of clippers.

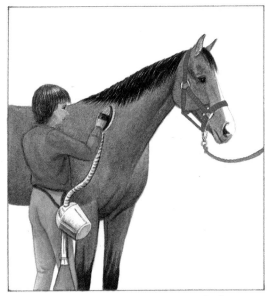

A non-rotary vacuum groomer with the container strapped to the waist – slower and harder work than the rotary type but quite good, and cheaper.

Feet

Even if you really haven't time to groom your horse properly, **always** pick out and inspect his feet and shoes at least once or twice a day. A stone, bottle-top or piece of broken glass, for example, can cause considerable bruising, and maybe wounding, if left jammed in the foot for long. Droppings left packed in the feet can encourage disease (thrush) by softening the horn, starting to decompose and creating an ideal environment for germs to breed. The same applies to dirty bedding, wet with urine, which gives off corrosive ammonia.

Outdoor horses on wet land can develop thrush as the water softens their horn and allows germs to establish. Soft feet can wear quickly, especially on the bulbs of the heels, so you need to check them daily.

You must also check the state of the shoes – whether they are still firm and well-fitting or are loose, have risen clenches or are so worn that they need replacing.

Risen clenches can tear open the opposite leg, seriously injuring it, and loose shoes can twist and break and injure the horse or bring him down. A lost shoe means you can only work your horse on soft ground and a loose one means you cannot work him at all until it has been tightened up or refitted by the farrier.

A daily clean-out and careful inspection can stop all these things happening or getting worse, and you can do it all in only five minutes. It could even save the lives of you and your horse by preventing a fall.

It's worth taking a folding hoof pick on rides. If the horse suddenly seems lame he may have picked up a stone, and you can remove it.

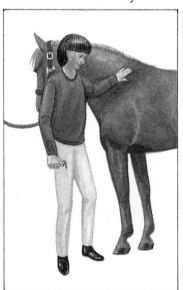

To pick up a front foot, stand facing the tail, stroke down from the shoulder to the fetlock and grasp the fetlock joint or hair. All at the same time, lean slightly on the horse to move his weight over, pull the fetlock up and say 'up'. Hold the hoof at the toe with the fetlock flexed so it is uncomfortable for him to lean on it.

 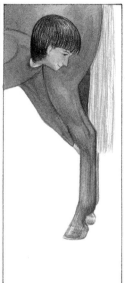  

To pick up a hind foot, standing facing the tail, stroke down from the hip, down the inside of the leg to the fetlock and lift and hold as for the front foot.

Have your 'holding' arm in *front* of the leg, as here, so if he kicks back (more likely than kicking forward) he won't pull you over.

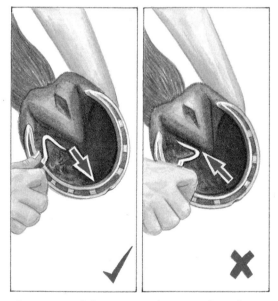

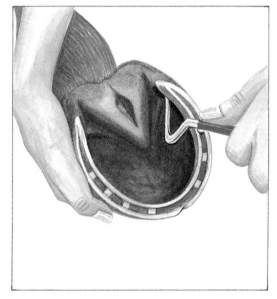

Scrape out debris, remembering side and centre grooves of frog. Work from heel to toe to avoid pushing dirt under the shoe at the heels, the loosest part.

To check for looseness, try (not *too* hard) to fit the end of the pick under the shoe heel and move it. If you can, it's loose and you need the farrier.

Quartering

This is done to tidy up the horse before work. His rugs, if worn, are folded forward and back to reveal his four quarters (hence the name) for grooming. This is done without fully removing his rugs. Round-the-girth fastenings can be left done up (except if any dried sweat on saddle and girth areas has to be removed – putting tack on top of dried mud or sweat can cause soreness).

Brush the horse lightly over with the dandy brush to remove bits of bedding, dried sweat, mud and stable stains. If the latter won't come off, do them with a damp sponge (the 'back end' sponge) or a water brush and rub with the rubber or an old towel afterwards.

Some people also 'lay' the mane and tail when quartering and put on a tail bandage for a while (if there is time before work) to further neaten the horse.

The feet are thoroughly picked out and the shoes carefully checked as working a horse with a loose shoe can be dangerous. If you've already mucked out, pick out the feet into a dung skip so you don't mess up the bed or floor, otherwise it doesn't matter. **Don't** pick out the feet in the yard or let the horse trail muck and bedding out in his feet as you, or someone else, will have to sweep it up. This makes unnecessary work.

Damp-sponge the eyes, nostrils and lips with the front-end sponge and do the sheath or udder, and dock area (between the buttocks and under the tail itself) with the back-end one. Dip them in water (**not** the horse's drinking water), 'front-end' sponge first, and squeeze till just damp. In winter, dry off with a rubber or an old towel.

Replace rugs or tack up for work.

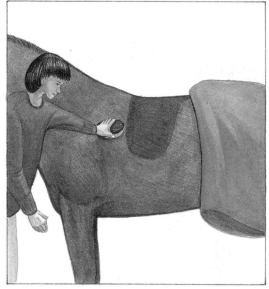

Fold the rugs back over the quarters and brush both sides of the front end first, properly known as the forehand. Don't forget the head and neck.

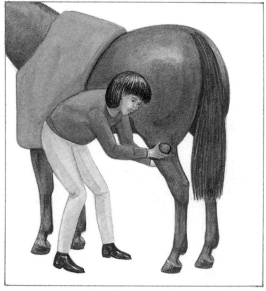

Fold the rugs forward over the forehand and do both sides of the hindquarters next. Then replace the rugs so the horse doesn't feel chilly.

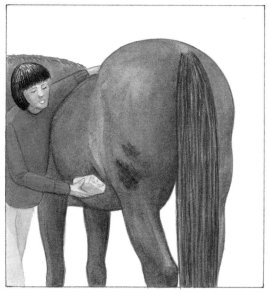

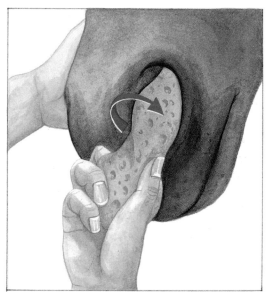

To remove stubborn stable stains (where the horse has lain on droppings) use the damped back-end sponge or water brush. Dry off with a rubber.

Gently insert the damp sponge in a roll into each nostril and twirl it round to clean out dirt. Remember to clean inside the little fold at the front.

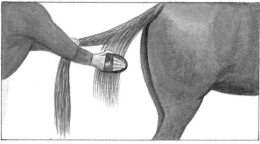

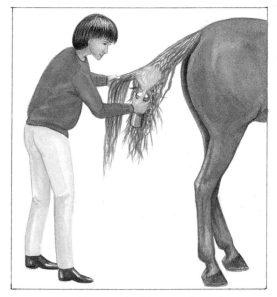

Throw the mane over the neck and brush back from the roots, lock by lock, with the body brush. Hold out the dock and brush down a lock of hair at a time.

For tangled hair or bedding in the tail spray with coat conditioner, leave a minute, then shake and carefully pick out debris and knots with your fingers.

Full grooming

Sometimes called 'strapping', this is the thorough grooming given usually after work when the horse is dry and warm, the dirt loosened and the skin warm and more easily cleaned.

First remove dried mud and sweat with the dandy brush – use it gently so as not to annoy the horse and make him difficult to groom in future. Be especially careful on sensitive, thin-skinned areas like the belly, head and inside legs.

Now for the hard work, the body-brushing. Hold the brush as shown in one hand and the metal curry comb in the other. It's easiest to groom the near side with your left hand and vice versa, but do change over if you get tired.

Hold your arm slightly bent at the elbow but stiff, and brush (in the direction the coat grows) by leaning your weight on the brush, not by pushing which is very tiring. Make about six longish strokes in one place. Don't slap the brush on the horse; put it on him and brush firmly, the object being to get through the hair to clean the skin.

Every two or three strokes clean the brush by drawing it firmly across the ridges of the curry comb, bristles down. Occasionally, tap the curry on its side on the floor to remove the dirt.

Obviously your method will change when doing head and legs, but the object is the same. Always brush back and down and do things in the same order from front to back so you don't forget parts like under mane and forelock, behind pasterns, inside ears and between legs.

Pick out the feet, sponge both ends, dust off the with the rubber, lay the mane and tail with the water brush – and you've finished.

Even using your weight properly, it's almost impossible to effectively clean a long winter coat with the body brush. It's for summer or clipped coats mainly.

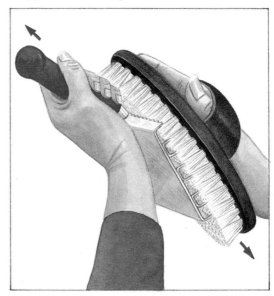

Holding the curry comb like this will stop you scratching the wrist of your brush hand with it when cleaning the body brush – quite painful!

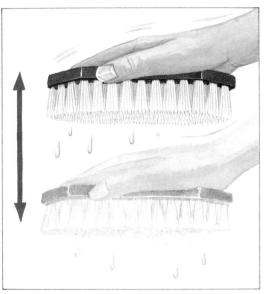

Dip the *tips* of the water brush bristles in water (not the drinking water) and shake it firmly *downwards* to remove excess water.

Place the damp brush on the far side of the neck, pushing the bristles into the roots of the mane, and brush down to 'lay' the mane to smooth it.

An old silk (not synthetic) scarf put over the body brush bristles for a final smooth-over will put a shine on the coat without creating static electricity.

Grooming is dusty work best done outside. A final smooth-down with the rubber will remove any dust which has landed on the coat since body-brushing.

Wisping

Wisping (or banging) is a type of muscle-building massage. The theory is that as you slap the wisp or pad on the horse, he flinches (and so works and develops his muscles) expecting the slap or bang. It is also said to squeeze natural oils out of the glands on to the skin and coat, giving a shine and helping protect them.

You must only wisp muscular areas, never bony or sensitive ones. The parts usually done are the topline of the neck, the muscles behind the shoulder/elbow and the hindquarters.

Wisping is usually done sometime after full grooming but can be performed any time on a healthy horse as its aim is massage and muscle development, not cleaning. It is not essential and many top yards don't do it now.

It seems to be a peculiarly British practice which foreigners find hilarious!

A leather pad stuffed hard with horse-hair or other material can replace a real wisp. Slap it on firmly but not too hard or you'll annoy or frighten the horse.

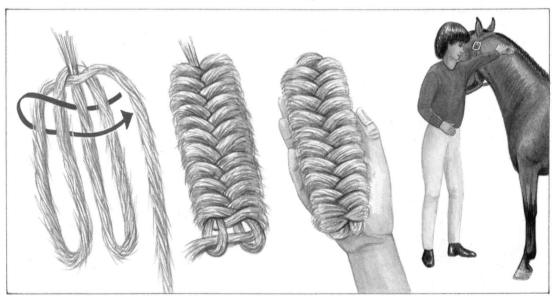

To make a wisp, firmly twist a rope of hay about 2m (6ft) long, form loops as shown and thread the rope in and out of the loops, keeping it tight and hard as you go.

Pass the end through the loops and tuck it in to finish off. It should just comfortably fit your hand. You use it with one hand, not two.

Cleaning the sheath

Geldings produce a dark, smelly, greasy discharge inside their sheaths, called smegma, which must be thoroughly washed away every fortnight or so, otherwise disease can occur. Also, the horse may stop letting down his penis to stale and urine will run all over his belly, causing a skin complaint. A clogged-up sheath is also very uncomfortable for the horse.

It can be very difficult to get the horse to let down his penis for cleaning, but when you spot that he has, talk soothingly to him and try to clean off any smegma or grit which has built up, particularly around the end of the penis where there may be a hard lump (called a 'bean') of smegma.

Most horses don't object to being cleaned here, but ask an expert to help you at first.

You need hand-hot water and mildly medicated soap to break down the greasy smegma, using your back-end sponge. You *must* rinse out the sheath *very thoroughly* afterwards, and dry off the outside and entrance with an old towel.

Finish by smearing liquid paraffin (*not* heater paraffin) inside the sheath to help prevent new smegma clinging and to soften it for easier removal.

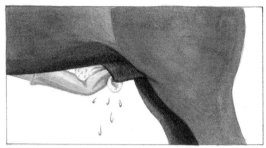

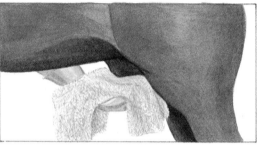

Gently put your well-soaped sponge right up inside the sheath and thoroughly wash all round. Rinse *very* thoroughly a few times and dry the outside skin.

You'll need hand-hot water, medicated soap, back-end sponge, liquid paraffin, a towel and, if you wish, fine rubber gloves.

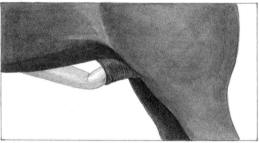

After rinsing, pour a little liquid paraffin into your hand and smear it all round well up and inside the sheath to soften new smegma and protect the skin.

The muddy horse

Whether your horse is stabled or kept out, there'll be times when he gets very muddy and needs extra attention.

If the mud is dry you need only to brush it off with the dandy brush; you could also use a rubber or plastic curry comb or a plastic 'pan-scrub' (see page 8). A cactus cloth can remove light mud. Whatever you use, brush or rub in the direction of the hair and from side to side to loosen the mud.

It is useless to brush wet or damp mud as you'll simply push it into the coat and make the horse sore. You must not put tack on top of mud, wet or dry, as it will soon rub your horse raw.

Some experts feel you should let mud dry and then brush it off. You can encourage it to dry by 'thatching' the horse and bandaging his legs. Thatching involves putting a thick layer of straw on his back and down his sides, kept on with an old rug. This warms the horse and dries him off quicker.

Other experts, and many vets, feel mud is best hosed or thoroughly rinsed off and *then* the horse thatched (or rugged with a 'breatheable'-fabric rug so the straw isn't needed) to dry him.

You can help dry the horse with handfuls of straw and old towels (stable rubbers are no use). A hand-held hairdryer is also very useful to speed things up. Follow the same safety precautions as for clipping machines.

It is particularly important in chilly or cold weather to dry the horse quickly. **Don't** leave him standing about, especially outdoors, but rug or thatch him, bandage his legs and lead him round or stand him in a stable. A box with an infra-red heater is very helpful (no rugs needed) in drying wet horses quickly, and these aren't expensive to run.

A thatched, bandaged horse. You can also use a rug with surcingles crossing under the belly if you fasten it snugly (not tightly).

A mesh anti-sweat rug can be used over straw or under an ordinary rug. Mesh dishcloths or pieces of old anti-sweat rugs under bandages dry legs well.

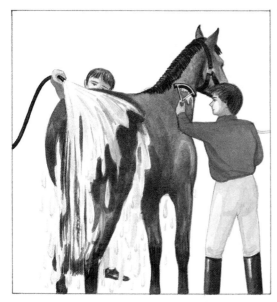

Hose the horse (best with warm water) from front to back (not the head) and remove excess water with a sweat scraper.

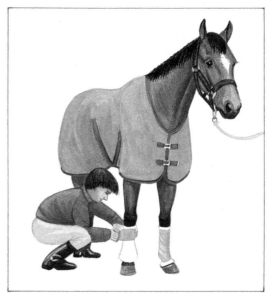

It's vital to dry the horse off quickly in chilly weather, especially loins, quarters, ears and legs, particularly heels and the backs of the pasterns.

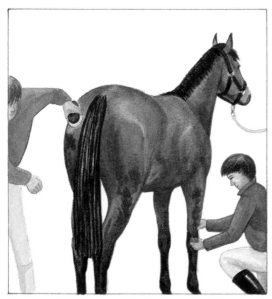

Remove dry mud from the body with the dandy brush, rubber or plastic curries or a plastic pan-scrub, working with the hair or from side to side.

To remove dry mud from mane and tail hair, roll strands back and forth firmly between your hands to avoid breaking the hairs with the dandy brush.

Shampooing

Shampooing is an effective way to clean a horse, with less work than grooming – but many people overdo it. Too much soap dries out the natural oils, makes the skin itchy and the horse likely to rub, and dulls the hair. Only shampoo if the horse is very greasy, otherwise a good rinse with plain warm water is safer and just as good. Notice how clean and silky your horse feels after he's been rained on.

Use special animal shampoo or baby shampoo, which is very mild. Don't 'rinse and repeat' – one application is plenty.

Do wash *and* rinse your horse in warm water. Some people rinse with cold and forget that the horse hates it as much as they would! Using cold water in winter is unkind and can really chill the horse.

If the weather is a bit chilly, wash the front half first leaving a rug over the hindquarters, then do the back and have a rug over the forehand *and* neck. Work quickly and then thatch or rug with an anti-sweat sheet or 'breatheable' rug, and bandage the legs. Or stand the horse unrugged in a heated box with a good bed, hay and water.

Chunky car sponges are ideal for shampooing but use one for soaping and one for rinsing as you'll never get all the soap out of the first one. Also, only use one of your buckets of water for soaping so you have plenty of clear water left for rinsing, which is *very* important.

If you thatch or use an anti-sweat sheet, remove them and rug up normally when the coat hair is still *slightly* damp, otherwise you'll get lines on it.

If it's chilly, the important thing is to dry the horse as quickly as you can, using towels, hairdryer etc., to avoid a chill.

You'll need lots of warm water, towels, rugs and bandages if chilly, car sponges, shampoo (maybe), and a hairdryer and sweat scraper would be helpful.

Wet the horse carefully (not the head) and work in the shampoo with a sponge in a circular motion. Use only one of your buckets of water for soaping.

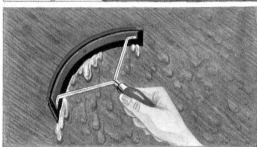

It's vital to rinse every bit of lather away as residues can cause soreness. Don't forget his underparts and the roots of his mane and tail.

Use the sweat scraper in the direction of the hair in long, sweeping strokes. The sides of your hands make a good substitute for a sweat scraper.

A shower-type instant water heater with a hose attached is a great help. Set at 40°C. You'll wonder how you ever managed without it! They aren't expensive.

An infra-red heater saves thatching, rugging and leading round and works quickly and cheaply. Leave door and window open for air, though.

Hot towelling

If it's too cold to shampoo and your horse is really dirty, give him a hot towel treatment instead. This is effective and safe and there's no risk of chilling the horse.

You need: a bucket of very hot (not boiling) water; rubber gloves; a thick soft towel; and, for a very greasy coat, shampoo; or, for a dry, dull coat, liquid human hair conditioner.

Add just a dash of shampoo or conditioner to the water, if required, and mix it in. Put the towel fully in the water then remove it and wring it out really hard.

Shake it out (which will cool it down a little) and lay it on the horse's coat for 4–5 seconds. The heat softens the hair and dirt. Then bundle up the towel and rub the hair firmly from side to side to remove the dirt. Finish by rubbing the hair smoothly in the direction in which it grows. Do this all over the horse.

To do the legs, wrap the towel round them and rub up and down. If the horse is very greasy, do each part twice.

The trick is to keep the water really hot so you may need to change it after one side. Of course, you can keep the horse's rugs on, just moving them about as you do different areas.

Part the mane and dock hair and do the roots of the hairs which can get greasy. Just wipe sensitive areas, like between buttocks, under the tail and around the sheath or udder with the warm, bundled-up towel.

It also works on the long mane and tail hair (wrap the hot towel round locks of hair and rub between your hands and then down), although even in winter you can wash the mane and tail in the usual way. Do the tail in a bucket and whirl it round after rinsing.

Use just a few drops of shampoo or conditioner and only if needed. You certainly won't scald the horse if you lay the flat towel on for a few seconds.

The heat loosens and softens the dirt. Rub firmly from side to side to remove it and finish by rubbing in the direction of the hair to smooth it.

Utility box

If you have room, a utility box or area is probably the most useful facility you can have in any yard.

You can use a spare loose box but it's better to have something a little bigger to give room for storage and to work around the horse. Perhaps you already have an under-cover area (or could make one in the form of a lean-to on the end of a row of boxes) which you could convert – a large garage without doors, a roomy car-port or disused small barn – anywhere you can stand the horse under cover and provide electric plug points, lighting, maybe an infra-red heater and non-slip flooring, for there will be no bedding in here.

The utility box can be used for grooming when it's too cold to groom outdoors so you don't fill the stable air with dust; trimming; clipping; perhaps veterinary treatment; plaiting up; shoeing – almost anything you can think of.

You will need shelves, cupboards or drawers in here, so that you have things to hand. It must also be big enough to allow the horse safely to swing about when tied up without damaging himself, fittings or equipment by bumping into them or treading on them.

The flooring can be of ridged rubber, which is a good safety precaution where electric machines are used.

A separate under-cover washing area can be a big advantage and does not necessarily have to be indoors. A hosepipe fitted to an instant water heater (professionally fitted) is ideal for washing down horses. Make sure that the water has a drainage outlet.

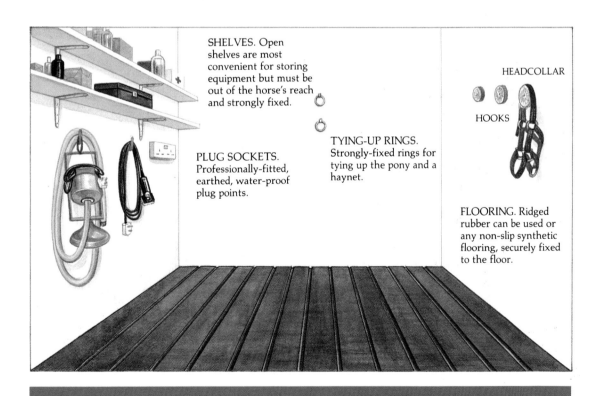

SHELVES. Open shelves are most convenient for storing equipment but must be out of the horse's reach and strongly fixed.

HEADCOLLAR

HOOKS

PLUG SOCKETS. Professionally-fitted, earthed, water-proof plug points.

TYING-UP RINGS. Strongly-fixed rings for tying up the pony and a haynet.

FLOORING. Ridged rubber can be used or any non-slip synthetic flooring, securely fixed to the floor.

Setting fair

The process of making your horse comfortable for the night is called 'setting fair'. This can also apply to bedding, but as far as grooming goes it means giving him a quick brush over to freshen him up, stimulate his skin, particularly if he wears clothing, picking out his feet again and maybe giving him a quick sponge.

Remove his clothing or fold the rugs backwards or forwards if it is cold and give him a quick, light brush over with the dandy brush to remove stable stains, dried mud (if he's been out), and dried sweat (although this should have been removed at full grooming earlier), then change to the body brush and tidy his mane, forelock and tail, untangling any knots and removing any bedding with your fingers.

Check his feet and shoes and pick them out into a dung skip. A quick sponge, especially in warm weather, will refresh the horse.

If the horse has had a tail bandage put on at full grooming, remove it now as it should not be left on all night, not least because if it comes off it could trip and injure him during the night.

If you haven't had time for a decent grooming earlier, you could do it now. Even though he's going to be lying down, it isn't a waste of time as the aim of grooming is to clean the horse and prevent a build-up of dirt.

Take his rugs off completely and either change them for night clothing to give the day rugs a chance to air, or replace them carefully, making sure they are comfortable for the night, neither too tight nor too loose.

Skip out the bed – there will be enough droppings in the morning as it is. Check water and hay. All this takes less than half an hour.